# INTERESTING INVERTEBRATES

## Also by Elaine Landau

# INTERESTING

# INVERTEBRATES

## A Look at Some Animals Without Backbones

BY ELAINE LANDAU

A FIRST BOOK
FRANKLIN WATTS
NEW YORK / LONDON / TORONTO / SYDNEY
1991

*For Eric and Sara*

Cover photograph copyright ©: Fred Bavendam

Photographs copyright ©: Animals Animals: pp. 13, 14 (both Mickey Gibson), 20, 31 (both Oxford Scientific Films), 22 (James D. Brandt), 26 (Michael Fogden), 27, 50 (both E.R. Degginger), 29 (Robert Maier), 32, 47 (both Breck P. Kent), 36, 38 (both Zig Leszczynski), 39 (Scott Johnson), 40 (O.S.F./David Shale), 45 (Keith Gillett), 54 (Raymond A. Mendez); Florida Department of Commerce, Division of Tourism: p. 16; Root Resources: pp. 23 (Anthony Mercieca), 51 (Don & Pat Valenti).

Library of Congress Cataloging-in-Publication Data

Landau, Elaine.
    Interesting invertebrates: a look at some animals without backbones/ by Elaine Landau.
        p.     cm.—(A First book)
    Includes bibliographical references and index.
    Summary: An introduction to the physical characteristics, habits, and natural environment of a variety of animals without backbones such as sponges, jellyfishes, sea anemones, worms, octopuses, and oysters.
    ISBN 0-531-20036-1
    1. Invertebrates—Juvenile literature.    [1. Invertebrates.]
I. Title.    II. Series.
QL362.4.L36  1991
592—dc20                   91-13700 CIP AC

# CONTENTS

# INTERESTING
# INVERTEBRATES

# Chapter 1

# INVERTEBRATES—
# ANIMALS WITHOUT
# BACKBONES

Quickly think of an animal. What comes to mind? Did you picture a dog, cat, horse, or tiger? Maybe you imagined a monkey or cow. Odds are that you didn't immediately think of a sponge, worm, or sea star.

Yet these are animals, too. Scientists call them invertebrates because they have no backbones. (The word for the bony segments of the backbone, or spinal column, is vertebrae).

It's difficult to imagine the many types of *invertebrates* that exist throughout the world. At present, scientists know that there are more than one million different kinds, or *species*, of animals without backbones.

Living things have been scientifically grouped into categories called phyla. Sometimes the animals within a given *phylum* (singular form of the word) may not seem very much alike. They may live in varied environments, and feed and move differently. They may also not be at all alike in size or form. Yet these animals have been grouped together because they are related. All animals within any given phylum can be traced back to a common ancestor.

# Chapter 2

# SPONGES

Sponges are animals whose *skeletons* have been used by people throughout the ages for bathing and scrubbing purposes. Sponges are grouped within the phylum Porifera, which means "pore bearers." They were not always recognized as animals. In fact, until about the middle of the nineteenth century, sponges were thought to be plants, or even nonliving objects.

Sponges live at the bottom of bodies of water. Although most sponges tend to dwell in warm ocean waters, some may also be found in lakes, rivers, and other fresh water areas. Unlike many other animals, sponges tend not to move about.

Sponges are among the oldest surviving animals on earth. *Fossils* of sponges dating back more than 500 million years have been found. All sponges do not look alike. These animals vary greatly in size and shape. Some sponges are tube-shaped. Others are round. Still others look like empty flower vases. A sponge growing over a rock or other object may take on that object's form. While some sponges are smaller than an inch (2.5 cm), others may be as large as 4 feet (1.2 m) wide.

Sponges also come in various colors—there are brilliant orange sponges as well as drab gray ones. Shiny yellow, red, purple, green, and brown sponges have been identified as well.

Sponges are capable of a remarkable process known as *regeneration*. This means that if a portion of the sponge's body is cut off or damaged, it will grow back. Scientists have conducted experiments with these animals to test the sponge's ability to regenerate. Tiny cells from a sponge were placed in a container of water. Soon, the cells joined together to form clusters. Eventually, a fully developed sponge was found in the container.

These are orange tube sponges. About five
thousand different types of sponges exist.

The gray sponges shown here were found near
the Cayman Islands in the Caribbean Sea.

A sponge does not have a mouth or teeth with which to eat its food. Instead, the surface of its body is covered with small pores called *ostia*. The animal's ostia allow water to flow through its body. As the water enters the animal, it carries tiny plants and animals into the sponge which serve as its food. Waste products are released by the sponge in a current of water that passes through a large opening, called an *osculum*, on the body's surface.

Various types of fish and other sea animals feed on sponges. A sponge cannot flee, bite, or hide in a shell from its *predators*. Yet, this seemingly passive animal is not completely defenseless. Numerous sponges have a somewhat hard crusty skeleton that may serve as a defense. Some sponges also produce toxic substances that poison their enemies. The poisonous substances secreted by some sponges may prove useful to researchers in developing new drugs. Scientists hope these substances may one day advance the treatment of cancer and other diseases.

Sponges have also been beneficial to humans in other ways. The sponge's skeleton

These sponges were taken from the sea. Some of
them will later be sold for cleaning purposes.

was once commonly used as a kitchen or bathroom cleaner. (Most sponges used today are artificially produced.) Sponge-fishing divers bring these animals up from the seafloor to a boat. After the sponge has died, its skeleton is thoroughly cleaned. The shells or skeletons of other tiny invertebrates that lived within the holes or cavities of the sponge are scrubbed away. Then the skeleton is treated and cut into a manageable shape before it is sold.

At one time, millions of sponges were sold by fishermen each year. However, due to water pollution and overfishing, the sponge industry has greatly declined. Today, natural sponges have become both costly and somewhat rare.

# Chapter 3

# JELLYFISH
# AND
# SEA ANEMONES

Jellyfish and sea anemones are invertebrates grouped within the phylum Cnidaria (previously known as Coelenterata). There are about 11,000 different species of Cnidarians, most of which may be found in ocean waters. Many of these animals are beautiful in appearance. Frequently, they are magnificently colored and have an elegant umbrella or bell-shaped form.

Animals within this phylum vary greatly in size. The smallest of these creatures are so tiny they can only be seen clearly under a microscope. Others may be huge—some jellyfish may weigh as much as a ton.

Animals grouped within this phylum are headless. Instead, they have a mouth at one

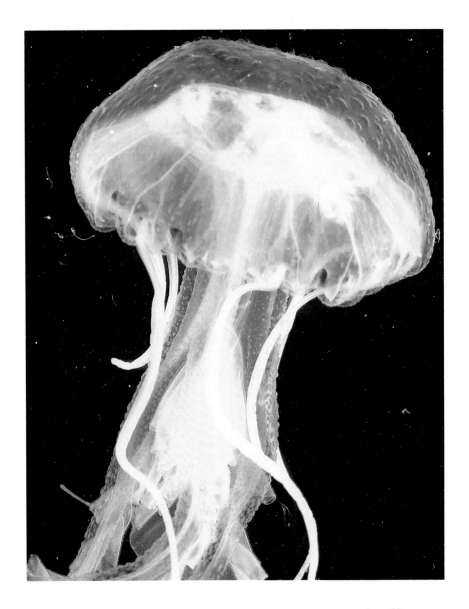

This jellyfish looks like a graceful umbrella
as it swims through the water.

end of their bodies. The animal's mouth is surrounded by long, stringlike extensions known as *tentacles*.

These invertebrates use their tentacles to capture food. The tentacles contain poison-bearing cells that sting when touched. As soon as these tentacles come in contact with the animal's prey, *toxins* are released. The venom paralyzes the prey so it cannot escape. Then the animal's tentacles draw its food into its mouth. The mouth leads directly to a large digestive cavity. There, the food is broken down and absorbed by the animal's body.

The jellyfish is an umbrella-shaped animal within this phylum. Some jellyfish are as small as pearls, while others may be over 7 feet (2.13 m) wide. A jellyfish doesn't have bones. It is made of a jellylike substance. Its body is supported by the water which it needs to live.

Different types of jellyfish vary in color. Often they are pale shades of pink, blue, orange, and other hues. A jellyfish swims with an umbrellalike motion. First, it opens its body. Then it quickly closes it shut again. This motion squeezes water out from under the jellyfish and propels the animal through the sea.

Some sea anemones, such as the
blue one shown here, may remain in the
same spot for long periods of time.
Although it is an animal, this
colorful sea anemone (left) looks like
a flower growing in the water.

People have been stung by jellyfish. In some types of jellyfish, the venom released can be extremely toxic to humans. There have been instances in which individuals have suffered extreme discomfort, and even death from a jellyfish sting.

Another invertebrate within the Cnidaria phylum is the sea anemone. The sea anemone has a tube-shaped body with numerous tentacles on top. Since the animal's body looks like a stem and its tentacles resemble flower petals, the sea anemone is sometimes mistaken for a plant. It was even named after a flower called the anemone, but appearance—and name—aside, the sea anemone is an animal!

Sea anemones may be pink, rose, blue, green, and other colors. They seem motionless because they are usually found fixed to a particular spot, such as a rock, but they are actually capable of very slow movement.

Sea anemones vary in size depending on the species. Some measure less than a quarter of an inch (0.6 cm). Others are over 3 feet (0.9 m) wide.

# Chapter 4

# WORMS

More than 15,000 different types of worms make up the phylum Annelida. These worms are grouped together because of their common traits. All the worms in this phylum have bodies made up of ringlike parts, or segments. Most also have movable bristles called *setae*. The setae help them to crawl.

Two other phyla consist entirely of worms as well. Worms within the various phyla are distinctly different from one another. For example, flatworms make up the phylum Platyhelminths. These worms have a very simple body structure. Some broadly shaped flatworms look like leaves. Other, narrower, species look like sticks of chewing gum.

This flatworm was photographed in a
Costa Rican rain forest. Flatworms are
found throughout the world.

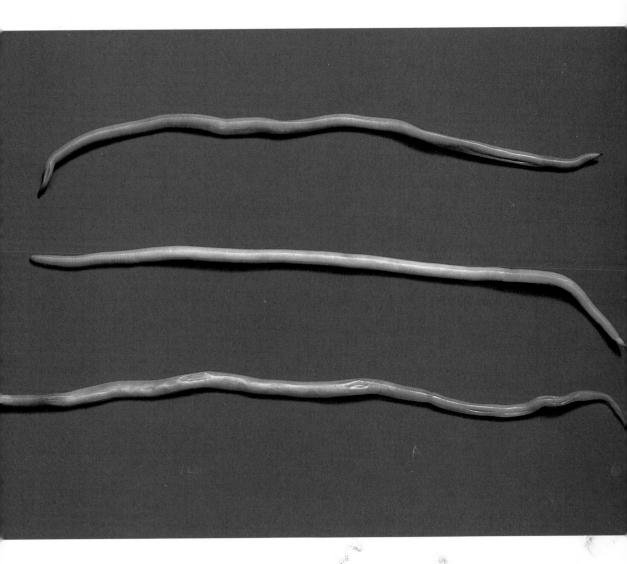

Parasitic roundworms have long slender bodies.
Some types cause diseases in humans,
animals, and plants.

More than 90,000 types of roundworms are grouped together in the phylum Nematoda. Unlike flatworms or worms with segmented bodies, roundworms have slim, round bodies. The roundworm's body tapers to a point at both its front and back ends. Some roundworms look like slender, moving, spaghetti strands.

Many worm species live independently in varied environments. Worms may be found in soil and water, as well as in decaying plant and animal matter. Frequently, they feed on *bacteria* as well as on tiny creatures that live around them. Some of these worms have proven especially useful to researchers in their laboratory experiments.

Other worm species are unable to exist on their own. These worms, known as *parasites*, feed off living plants and animals. The plants and animals that support parasitic worms are called hosts.

The leech is a worm with a ringed, or segmented, body. Leeches vary in size. Some are less than an inch (2.5 cm) long, while others may grow to 12 inches (30 cm). There are dif-

Leeches, like the one shown here,
live in damp or wet areas.

ferent colored leeches, too. These worms may be black, red, or brown. Some leeches even have stripes or spots. Leeches do not have eyes as we know them. However, near the front end of the worm are groups of cells that can detect light.

There are actually two types of leeches. Some eat dead plant and animal matter. Others live as parasites, feeding off the blood and tissues of animals and humans. Both the front and back ends of the leech have a round body part called a sucker. The leech's front sucker contains the worm's mouth. Some leeches also have small teeth.

Parasitic leeches attach themselves to their human or animal host with their back suckers. They use their front suckers and small teeth to create an opening in the host's skin. Then they draw out the host's blood. The blood flows out easily, because leeches give off a blood-thinning substance called hirudin.

Once the leech has its fill of blood, it drops off. Leeches generally don't remain on a single host. They continually search out new feeding sources. But even if they don't find a new host

A parasitic leech feeds on a human's blood.

Since fishermen often use earthworms as bait,
they are sometimes called fishworms.

immediately, they may still survive. The leech's digestive tract contains pouches that hold enough blood to last the worm for months.

Years ago, leeches were often used in the practice of medicine. At the time, doctors believed that certain illnesses could be cured by drawing off their patient's "bad" blood.

Earthworms are a different type of segmented worm. As these worms feed on dead plant matter within the soil, they are extremely helpful to the environment. By breaking down decayed matter as they feed, earthworms help release important nutrients into the soil. Since the earthworm only eats a small amount, many nutrients are left to enrich the earth. This process benefits growing crops.

Earthworms are also helpful in other ways. As they burrow through the soil, they create holes in the dirt. These holes allow air, vital to plant growth, to enter the soil. Earthworms are also a valuable food source for many birds. In addition, fishermen use these worms for bait.

# Chapter 5

# SEA STARS, SEA URCHINS, AND SAND DOLLARS

Ocean invertebrates with a hard prickly outer covering, or skin, make up the phylum Echinodermoda. One such animal is the sea star (also called starfish). There are over 1,600 species of sea stars throughout the world's oceans. These invertebrates look like stars with their round bodies from which five or more pointed armlike growths extend.

Along the bottom of each arm, the sea star has rows of small tube feet. Each foot has a suction cup at its tip. These cups allow the animal to move slowly along the ocean bottom or seashore.

The sea star's tube feet are also helpful in obtaining food. Sea stars most often feed on

This is a large African sea star.
Various types of sea stars are
found in the world's oceans.

shellfish such as clams and oysters. By placing its tube feet on both sides of a clam's shell and pulling hard, the sea star can pry open the shell and eat the soft-bodied animal inside.

As is true of some other invertebrates, a sea star is able to regenerate. If it loses one of its arms, it can grow a new one.

Another type of ocean invertebrate within the phylum Echinodermoda is the sea urchin. This is a round sea animal with long movable spines extending out from its body. Beneath the sea urchin's pointed spines is a hard limestone shell that supports and protects the animal's delicate body.

The sea urchin's sharp spines are essential to its survival. They provide protection from enemies. The spines are also used for travel. Sea urchins move along the ocean's bottom on the tips of their spines.

The sea urchin's mouth is centered on the underside of its body. These ocean invertebrates have five teeth with which to chew their food. They feed on decaying matter, seaweed, and tiny living animals.

A sea star in search of a meal
pulls open a clam.

The sea urchin's long spines sometimes
look like a flower's petals.

The sand dollar may look like a coin
lost in the sand. This small animal's
mouth is on the underside of its body.

Sand dollars are sea animals that look somewhat like silver dollars. They are slim animals that have flat round bodies between 2 and 4 inches (5–10 cm) wide. On the upper surface of the sand dollar are its rows of breathing holes. They go from the center to the outer edges and are shaped like five petals of a flower.

Sand dollars are covered with short, slender spines. The sand dollars use their spines for travel as well as to dig themselves into the sand. These invertebrates usually remain partly hidden beneath the sand. There they feed on small bits of plant and animal matter.

# Chapter 6

# OCTOPUSES AND OYSTERS

Soft-bodied animals that are often enclosed within a shell make up the phylum Mollusca. About 110,000 species of these invertebrates are known to us. Nearly 40,000 are now extinct. Scientists learned about them through fossil remains. Today living mollusks can be found in such varied environments as deep seas and high mountain areas. No matter where these animals live, though, their bodies must remain moist in order for them to survive.

The octopus is classified within the phylum Mollusca. This animal has two well-developed eyes, eight long, powerful arms, jaws like a parrot's beak, and three hearts. The octopus also has the most advanced brain of any known invertebrate. Unlike most mollusks, the octopus doesn't have an outer shell. Instead, a tough covering called a mantle protects the animal's body and gives it shape.

An octopus does not use its arms to swim through the water. Instead, the animal sucks water into its body, then squeezes the water out through an opening in its head called a siphon. The force of the expelled water propels the octopus in a backward motion through the ocean.

In times of danger, the octopus can also squirt a dark liquid from its siphon. The fluid acts as a defense for the animal. It hides the octopus from humans, and from sharks and other predators looking for a meal.

The octopus depends on *camouflage* to protect itself in another way as well. When the animal becomes frightened, small amounts of colored material connected to its nervous system are released. This allows the octopus to change color. The octopus may become striped or perhaps turn blue, gray, purple, red, or another color. In order to remain hidden, the octopus often turns a color that blends in with its surroundings.

Octopuses, such as the one shown here,
are sometimes also called devilfish.

An octopus makes good use of its strong arms in catching food. Its diet usually consists of such shellfish as lobsters, clams, crabs, and mussels. Some octopuses release a poison that serves to paralyze their prey.

Of the fifty known types of octopuses, most have bodies about the size of an orange. Some larger species also exist. Giant octopuses have been found in waters near the northwestern coast of the United States. These animals may weigh close to 100 pounds (45 kg).

Oysters are also grouped within the phylum Mollusca. These are headless, soft-bodied animals that are protected by a hard outer shell. They are often found on the ocean bottoms of quiet shallow waters. Oysters may be especially plentiful in warm water.

The oyster's body rests in the bottom portion of its shell. The top half serves as a cover. Although the oyster usually keeps its shell slightly open, it will quickly snap it shut when an enemy approaches. An oyster's shell is its only defense against predators.

Since oysters and other mollusks do not

Oysters are often found in calm,
shallow, warm waters.

have lungs, the animals use featherlike gills to breathe. Oysters also use their gills to filter microscopic plants and animals from the water toward their mouth.

The oyster's mantle—an organ that lines its shell—is extremely important to the animal's survival. The mantle produces substances that form the oyster's shell. As the animal grows, the mantle continues to secrete fluids to extend the protective covering.

Sometimes, a grain of sand may accidentally enter an oyster's shell. The grain may rub against the oyster and irritate its body. In response, as a sort of defense mechanism, the mantle secretes the same fluid used to make the oyster's shell. Layers of this material continue to coat the tiny sand grain. Eventually, a pearl is formed.

Oysters are eaten by sea stars, fish, crabs, and other sea animals. Oysters are also considered a delicacy by some humans. People have eaten oysters for centuries. They were even enjoyed by the early Romans in ancient times. Every year, people around the world still consume millions of these animals.

# Chapter 7

# CRAYFISH AND ANTS

Animals that have legs with joints as well as an outer protective skeleton are grouped within the phylum Arthropoda. The crayfish, a freshwater invertebrate that looks something like a small lobster, is a member of this phylum. The crayfish thrives in lakes and rivers throughout much of the world. This invertebrate rarely grows larger than 6 inches (15 cm) long and may be light pink, orange, brown, dark green, or bluish black.

The crayfish's body is shielded from harm by its hard shell. This protective covering is called an *exoskeleton*. Crayfish have a total of sixteen legs—of which ten are used for walking. The other six are used for handling food.

The crayfish, also known as the crawfish,
is highly adaptable. If one of its legs or
claws is lost, it grows a new one.

The animal's two front legs are actually large, sharp claws. A crayfish's claws are crucial to its survival. They are used for catching prey.

Crayfish feed mainly on smaller fish, snails, and newly hatched insects. During much of the day, a crayfish may remain hidden under a rock or deep within a burrow. After dark, it frequently comes out to hunt for food.

Ants and other insects are also grouped within the phylum Arthropoda. Scientists believe that more than 10,000 different types of ants exist. Large numbers of ants live together in groups known as colonies. That's why ants are often known as *social insects*.

Ant colonies vary in size. While some are made up of small ant groups, others may have millions of inhabitants. Every ant in a colony has a specific job to do.

Each ant colony has one or more queens. The queen ant lays the eggs. Other ants called workers provide the queens with food and protection. All the worker ants within a colony are female. A male ant's only job is to mate with the queens. Male ants tend not to live very long.

The female worker ants make certain that the colony thrives and grows. They tend the young and bring in food. These ants also do necessary repairs to keep the nest in good condition.

No two ant species are identical, but many are alike in some ways. As is true of other invertebrates within their phylum, an ant's body is shielded by a hard, somewhat brittle, outer covering. The ant's exoskeleton protects its vital organs. Although all ants are similar in body structure, they vary in size. Some species are only a quarter of an inch (0.6 cm) long. Others measure over an inch (2.5 cm) in length.

Various types of ants live in different ways. Some are hunters who roam the countryside searching for insects to eat. Other ants attack neighboring ant colonies to steal their young. When the stolen ants mature, they work in the new colony. These ants maintain the nest, as well as bring back food to the ants who had earlier captured them.

Harvester ants gather seeds from the ground. They carry the seeds back to their colony to be stored in special compartments.

Harvester ants are hard-working seed
gatherers. About ten thousand different types
of ants are found throughout the world.

These small insects are capable of carrying heavy loads. In fact, ants can pick up loads many times their own body weight. By keeping an abundant food supply in their nests, harvester ants survive lean times.

Other types of ants are known as dairying ants. These ants live off a rich, sweet fluid they obtain from other insects.

With the exception of freezing cold regions, ants populate nearly every type of land environment. They are especially abundant in the tropics. Ants exist in various types of shelters. These include underground tunnels and mounds of earth, as well as the inside of trees and the hollow parts of plants. Ants are truly remarkable invertebrates.

# GLOSSARY

*Bacteria*—simple one-celled organisms

*Camouflage*—a disguise or behavior that is used by an animal to hide itself or deceive an enemy

*Exoskeleton*—a hard protective outer covering such as a shell

*Fossil*—traces of an animal or plant preserved in the earth's crust

*Invertebrate*—an animal that lacks a backbone

*Osculum*—the opening in a sponge's body through which water flows out of the animal

*Ostia*—the tiny openings on a sponge's body through which water enters

*Parasite*—a plant or animal that lives off another living plant or animal

*Phylum*—one of the major divisions of the animal kingdom

*Predator*—a person or animal that preys on another

*Regeneration*—a regrowth process through which damaged organs and tissues are replaced

*Setae*—movable bristles found on worms

*Skeleton*—the supporting framework of an animal

*Social insect*—an insect, such as an ant, that lives within a structured community

*Species*—a category of animals sharing certain common traits

*Tentacle*—a long slender body part extending from an animal; in some animals, they are the organs of touch or motion, or have other functions

*Toxin*—a substance that is poisonous when introduced into the body

# FOR FURTHER READING

Craig, Janet. *Amazing World of Spiders*. Mahwah, N.J.: Troll, 1989.

Fine, John Christopher. *Creatures of the Sea*. New York: Atheneum, 1989.

Johnson, Sylvia A. *Hermit Crabs*. Minneapolis: Lerner, 1989.

MacFarlane, Ruth B. Alford. *Making Your Own Nature Museum*. New York: Watts, 1989.

O'Toole, Christopher. *Discovering Ants*. New York: Bookwright Press, 1986.

Selsam, Millicent E. *Where Do They Go? Insects in the Winter*. New York: Scholastic, 1984.

# INDEX

Page numbers in *italics* refer to illustrations.

# ABOUT THE AUTHOR

Elaine Landau received her B.A. degree in English and journalism from New York University and a master's degree in library and information science from Pratt Institute.

Ms. Landau has worked as a newspaper reporter, an editor, and a youth services librarian. She has written more than thirty-five books for young people. Ms. Landau lives in Sparta, New Jersey.